God's People Revived

An Account of the Spontaneous Revival at Asbury College in February 1950

Edited by

Henry C. James

First Fruits Press
Wilmore,
Kentucky
c2018

God's people revived : an account of the spontaneous revival at Asbury College in February 1950 by Henry C. James
First Fruits Press, ©2018
Previously published by the Seminary Press, 1957.

ISBN: 9781621718529 (print), 9781621718574 (digital), 9781621718581 (kindle)

Digital version at https://place.asburyseminary.edu/
firstfruitsheritagematerial/160

James, Henry C.
   God's people revived : an account of the spontaneous revival at Asbury College in February 1950 / compiled and edited by Henry C. James. -- Wilmore, Kentucky : First Fruits Press, ©2018.
            83 pages : illustrations, portraits ; 21 cm.
            God's people -- A needy people -- A praying people -- A Spirit-filled people -- A witnessing people.
            Reprint. Previously published: Wilmore, KY. : Seminary Press, 1957.
            ISBN: 9781621718529 (pbk)
            1. Revivals--Kentucky--Wilmore. 2. Asbury College (Wilmore, Ky.). I. Title.

BV3775.W55 J35 2018   269

Cover design by Jon Ramsay

asburyseminary.edu
800.2ASBURY
204 North Lexington Avenue
Wilmore, Kentucky 40390

First Fruits
THE ACADEMIC OPEN PRESS OF ASBURY SEMINARY

First Fruits Press
The Academic Open Press of Asbury Theological Seminary
204 N. Lexington Ave., Wilmore, KY 40390
859-858-2236
first.fruits@asburyseminary.edu
asbury.to/firstfruits

God's People Revived

An Account Of The

SPONTANEOUS REVIVAL

At Asbury College

In February 1950

Compiled and Edited

by

Henry C. James

January 1957

INTRODUCTION

There is a two-fold purpose for the compiling of this booklet: namely, that those interested who have had only thumb-nail sketches of this spontaneous movement of the Spirit of God upon the campus of Asbury College may be able to read the full account and that the knowledge of these events may enrich the spiritual lives of the readers.

However, it would be attempting the impossible to try to put on paper all that took place at Asbury College from Thursday, February 23, at nine o'clock in the morning to Wednesday, March 1, 1950. Dr. Holland, a faculty member, expressed the difficulty thus: "No artist could paint the picture, no pen describe it, and it eludes the lens of the camera. The full conception of it must await the revelation of the Eternal Day."

The material for this booklet has been obtained from newspaper articles loaned by friends, and from accounts in the Asbury Collegian and the Pentecostal Herald, furnished by the libraries of Asbury College and Asbury Theological Seminary. The compiler of this booklet wishes also to express his indebtedness and appreciation to friends for their encouragement and valuable suggestions.

Those of us who were fortunate enough to be present during this mighty rising tide of prayer and faith could never be the same afterward. These events will live on forever within the souls of all those who received light and help from this refreshing movement of the Holy Spirit.

It is hoped that this compilation of facts may be as much of a blessing to the readers as the actual events were to those who witnessed this spiritual awakening of God's people!

II Chronicles 7:14 "*If my people which are called by my name, shall humble themselves and pray, and seek my face, and turn from their wicked ways; then will I hear from heaven, and will forgive their sin, and will heal their land."*

Acts 4:31 "*And when they had prayed, the place was shaken where they were assembled together; and they were all filled with the Holy Ghost, and they spake the word of God with boldness."*

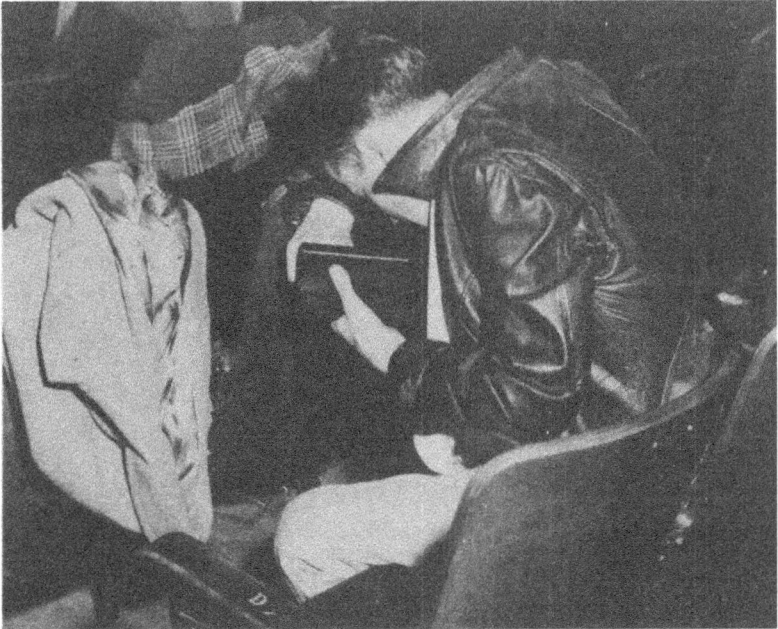

"People knelt alone in prayer everywhere in the auditorium; others sac quietly weeping or remained quiet as the Spirit dealt with them . . . . "

CHAPTER ONE
God's People

"If my people which are called by my name. . ."

THE SCHOOL

Asbury College was founded in 1890 by Dr. John Wesley Hughes, a member of the Kentucky Conference of the Methodist Church South. It was named in honor of Bishop Francis Asbury, who led in the organization of Bethel Academy on a spot about three miles from Wilmore on the banks of the Kentucky River. This academy, founded in the early 1800's but now extinct, was the oldest church school in Kentucky and the second oldest in America. Although named for Bishop Asbury, the college is interdenominational, with an average of about thirty denominations represented, and is supported by individual contributions.

The purpose of the school is not only to train students for the various professions but also to lead them to become so established in a Christian experience that they will effectively serve God both while they are here and after they have departed.

Approaching the front of Hughes Auditorium on the campus, one will see carved in concrete blocks set in red bricks these words: "Free salvation for all men and full salvation from all sin" and "Follow peace with all men and holiness without which no man shall see the Lord." These inscriptions present the spiritual foundation upon which this school has stood over these many years. From its founding, the college has adhered to the Wesleyan doctrine of Scriptural holiness as a separate work of grace, subsequent to regeneration.

From the early days of its history to the present, this institution has been a place of revivals, of which have been phenominal in their power and extent. However, those who have witnessed some of these great awakenings affirm that nothing comparable to the revival which began on February 23, 1950, has ever before been seen on this campus.

IMPRESSIONS OF THE REVIVAL

The great revival of 1950 impressed me in many different ways. One of the most unusual phases was the suddenness with which the revival began.

Thursday morning at chapel, Mr. and Mrs. Dee Cobb were in charge. The service was a good one and enjoyed by students and faculty. When the Cobbs were bringing the service to a close, I leaned over to Dr. Hamann and said, "I feel that I must give the students an opportunity to give some testimonies. Something will break loose if I don't."

I made my way hurriedly to the platform; and before I could say a word, there were several students on their feet to give their testimonies. The Holy Spirit descended so suddenly and powerfully that we all felt His presence in a way never before experienced. For the next four or five days nearly all of the time some one was praising the Lord, either in song or testimony.

Dr. J. B. Kenyon, College Dean

Let me lose myself and find it, Lord, in Thee,
May all self be slain,
My friends see only Thee,
Though it cost me grief and pain,
I will find my life again,
If I lose myself I'll find it, Lord, in Thee."

After this song was sung by Rev. and Mrs. Cobb, he preached on the subject, "BUT I WHOLLY FOLLOWED THE LORD MY GOD." Here is what he felt at the time:

When my wife and I sang our duet, "Let Me Lose Myself," just before I was to speak, the Holy Spirit seemed to specially bless our hearts as we sang and to apply the truth of the song to the hearts of those who listened. A kind of holy hush settled down in the brief interim after the close of the duet and the moment I was to begin my message. At that moment Bob Barefoot (as I recall) stood to his feet for a word of praise about a prayer meeting which a group of the boys had the night before where a number of fellows found the Lord. He suggested this would be an appropriate time for them to give a word of testimony, which they did. Others rose to their feet for testimony, and this would have continued had not the one in charge of the service stepped forward to say he thought time should be given for the speaker to bring his message.

Sensing something unusual about the atmosphere of the hour, I was somewhat reluctant to speak, but felt led of the Lord to read my Scripture and bring an abbreviated message. The Spirit seemed to indite as I preached. It is difficult to find words to express the "feeling" of that hour. It was as though an electric shock moved over the whole place, and there came such a sense of the presence of God that one felt almost as though he could just reach out and touch Him. From where I stood I would probably best describe it as something like a gentle breeze sweeping across a broad field of wheat. Everyone seemed moved, tears started down some cheeks, and a rapture of delight stirred some to gentle laughter. All over the auditorium young people were standing. Then some, weeping, started to the altar. From then on it was like feasting in the heavenlies.

Rev. Dee Cobb, Evangelist of the Methodist Church

If I were required to express the most significant thing about that great spiritual movement, I should say it was the genuine sincerity on the part of all who participated.

The revival was not planned by man or the college; it was not brought about by organization, any great evangelist or any outstanding human personality or personalities. It came, in my judgment, as the result of the sincere prayers of the faculty, officers, and the student body. It was not promoted by any great preaching.

No effort was made on the part of the faculty or of the administration to superimpose the revival spirit upon the student body. We wanted only the will and the work of God.

For several weeks the prayer life of Asbury College had been deepening. Groups of students had assembled for fasting and prayer with the faith and expectation that "If my people which are called by my name shall humble themselves, and pray, and seek my face, and turn from their wicked ways; then will I hear from heaven, and will forgive their sins, and will heal their land" (II Chronicles 7:14).

The symptoms which were discernible came to fruition on Thursday morning, February 23, at the chapel service at nine o'clock. From that moment, for 118 hours there was continuous prayer and praise.

So mighty was the presence of the Holy Spirit in that chapel service that the students could not refrain from testimony. The guest speaker had little opportunity for His message. The floodgates of heaven lifted and God moved into our midst as I have never before witnessed. The Holy Spirit fell upon the entire audience and everything broke loose. Testimonies were followed by confessions, confessions by crowded altars, crowded altars gave place to glorious spiritual victories, and this in turn to more testimonies. Thus it ran for several days. Wave after wave of glory swept the vast audiences; triumph after triumph took place at the altar. At times, the Divine presence was so pronounced that one could gather some conception of what St. Paul must have experienced when he was caught up into the Third Heaven.

The high point in that Thursday morning service was the confession period. This was such a sacred experience, when student after student laid bare his heart in confessing the wrongs done and asking forgiveness, that it seems out of place to narrate it. This, however, deepened the conviction and students plead with fellow students to confess and repent and find God. This proved to be the most effective kind of preaching, and the great altar, which overflowed to the rows of chairs, was filled again and again. Indeed the tremendous altar services, the constant flow of testimonies over the public address system, and the ecstatic joy of the audience went on simultaneously; but it all blended into the harmony of a Heavenly symphony.

The service continued uninterrupted through the day and into the night. There could be no dismissal. Long after the midnight hour the crowd remained. The suggestion that the people go to their rest and return in the morning brought small response. About three hundred people remained all night in the chapel to pray.

The writer went to the auditorium about six o'clock Friday morning and found the services still going on. Almost immediately thereafter the crowds began to assemble. They seemed to have been drawn by a mighty magnet -- indeed they were. Christ was lifted up and He drew them.

All day Friday the tide kept rising. A long line of students stood awaiting their turn to testify. For three days there was never a time when there were not people waiting in line to give their testimonies. I have seen the flood waters of rivers, and have read of breaking dams releasing almost unlimited reservoirs of water to augment the flood which was beyond its banks; so I can faintly visualize the lifting of the floodgates of Heaven, releasing His immeasurable flood of grace and glory. Something tremendous struck the audience Friday night. Far into the morning, God was banking His glory mountain high.

Thus, the services continued through Saturday, Sunday, and Monday and Tuesday. It was advised that we attend the various churches of Wilmore Sunday morning. Most of the group did, but the prayer chain, which was unplanned, was unbroken.

No services were announced for Sunday morning. In fact, no services were announced since Thursday morning. An irresistible power drew the multitudes. They came from far and near, and packed the large auditorium before service time. Sunday afternoon and night were truly great services. They were still going in full force at two o'clock Monday morning. Many refused to leave the auditorium at all. The Dean permitted the young men to remain while the ladies went to their dormitories, where prayer services continued under the direction of their monitors. Meetings were held each night during the succeeding week with scores of people seeking the Lord.

Everyone conceded that God was the leader of it all!

Dr. W. W. Holland, Chairman of Division
of Philosophy and Religion

Impression of other faculty members given in the revival edition of the Asbury Collegian.

"I shall forever praise the Lord for what this revival at Asbury has meant to the student body, the faculty, the community, and the nation. My prayer is that the revival fires will continue to sweep this nation and the world, for the salvation of men is our only hope from total destruction. This was a time of heart-searching in my own life, and how I praise Him for meeting my need. As director of the glee club, I am so grateful that we are all in one accord as never before; and I believe that God will use us in a mighty way as we go out to witness for Him."

Marvin Dean, Glee Club Director

"One of the most significant things in this revival has been the reality of God's presence. Many times religion is merely a projection of the imagination -- without reality. God is His own evidence--and this has given us an experience we can know is real."

Leon Fisher, Psychology Department

"This revival is the moving of the Holy Spirit upon our hearts to bring us to the realization that God has a way out of this world of confusion if we will commit ourselves to His leadership."

Virginia Hayes, Language Department

"The attention of the whole nation has been drawn to Asbury by this revival. 'For unto whomsoever much is given, of him shall much be required; and to whom men have committed much, of him they will ask the more' (Luke 12:48)."

Dr. D. C. Corbitt, Head of History Department

"The success of this revival can be measured not so much by its horizontal spread to other places as by the depth to which it has gone in each individual heart."

Mrs. D. C. Corbitt, Language Department

"In my opinion the present revival is most nearly akin to the experience of the early disciples on that day of Pentecost that I have heard of in modern time. I believe that this revival is God's answer to the crying need of the world and that it has come at an opportune moment in the life of Asbury that the students who are going out will go with lighted torches to kindle revival fires throughout the world. I have been particularly impressed with the spirit of spontaneity which has characterized the revival. Another feature has been the sense of clarity of direction which has come from the Holy Spirit with a minimum of human guidance and instruction."

Dr. A. T. Puntney, Head of English Department

When the news was made known that a religious revival was in progress at Asbury College, Wilmore, Kentucky, the Community News editor decided to make the trip to the college.

"I don't know if the trip was made out of curiosity, willingness to see this thing for myself, or to try to find an explanation for it.

Saturday afternoon, accompanied by photographer Harold Rogers, I made the trip to the college. As we approached the campus, it appeared deserted. No activity of any kind was noticeable. When we entered the grounds of the college the sounds of singing could be heard. Pulling up in front of one of the buildings, we inquired if the revival was still in progress. A young man replied, "Yes, praise the Lord, it is."

The expression was made with such obvious and deep sincerity it took me by surprise.

We climbed the stairs to Hughes Auditorium, the scene of the revival. It was already in its third day. As we entered the building there could be seen a cluster of young people gathered about the front center portion of the meeting hall.

Not being accustomed to the surroundings or the activities, Rogers and I decided to sit in the rear of the auditorium. For approximately 20 minutes we sat there watching as the students gave vent to their beliefs.

I have never seen such happy people. An observer could not help but notice the youthfulness of the gathering. There was much singing of hymns, prayers, testimonials, and confessions. Periodically, some of the students would mount the platform to give public testimony, or to reaffirm their faith in God. To be impressed by such scenes the revival had to be witnessed.

Soon we were approached by one of the students of the college. He asked us if we would care to take part in the ceremonies being conducted. Hesitatingly, Rogers and I told him we were there to find the reasons for this marathon religious demonstration to God. Never witnessing anything like it before, we wanted to see how it was being conducted.

For close to an hour this young man, a native of New York City, told us of his finding God. He related his story with such obvious sincerity one couldn't help but be struck by it. His faith in God was a wonder to behold. Here was a young man in the material world of today apparently oblivious to it all. He seemed not bothered or worried about such things that appear to be the major problems of the young.

During our talk the revival continued at its spirited pace. People kept coming into the auditorium and joining in the singing and praying.

It had been our intention to remain there approximately 15 minutes, get a story, perhaps a picture or two, then leave. But it proved so appealing to stay there and watch this almost unbelievable demonstration of religion, we stayed for a much longer period of time.

As for the young fellow we talked with, I have never seen anyone so happy. He gave the appearance of actually glowing with hapiness. A warmth that you wished could be catching. Here was a sight to put envy into the heart of anyone.

He told us how the revival had started. One of the students, Barefoot by name, had offered a testimonial during one of the religious meetings held regularly during the school period. From there the spirit of the movement was reflected throughout the student body, and the revival began.

Throughout the talk the Asbury student conversing with Rogers and me kept repeating his convictions. It was his goal to go out into the missionary field and preach. For the better part of our talk he tried to tell us of his feelings. Words apparently could not do the task. All one had to do was to look at this student and become convinced that he had found something to alter the course of his life.

Patiently and carefully he told us of his conversion. He explained his attitude prior to receiving his beliefs. Cynicism and disbelief had been his chief fortes when he enrolled in Asbury College. The firm religious beliefs of his fellow-students made him give long thought to the idea of a good and loving God. Friday, the second day of the movement, he said his faith became firm, unwavering, and permanent. When he found his faith, he said nothing else mattered.

Youth was the mainstay of the whole movement. Although there were a few older people scattered throughout the gathering, it was very obvious that it was predominantly the students of the college who were the main participants.

Fanaticism had no part in it. There were no great emotional or theatrical displays. Those who got up in front of the microphone gave vent to their beliefs. Sympathy and understanding of the audience was always with them. It was one of the most moving experiences I have ever witnessed.

Reflecting, the thought occured to me that perhaps more of this is the answer to the war-racked world. When youth returns to God, it is hard to see how militarists can convince them that war is so necessary.

Whatever the answer, the most obvious thing gleaned from this religious movement at Asbury College is that it beats an armament race anytime.

Edwin Leavens, editor Community News
Lexington's Weekly Paper

CHAPTER TWO

A Needy People

" . . . shall humble themselves and pray, and seek my face, and turn from their wicked ways; then will I hear from heaven, and will forgive their sin, and will heal their land."

MANY NEEDS

Some people might question whether a revival would be necessary in a school like Asbury, where there is a Christian atmosphere and where standards are high. However, although the majority of the students, with the faculty, have an interest in the spiritual welfare of others, there are sometimes young people who may be here for the full four years and never experience salvation. Wherever there are Christian people, there are always those various and desperate needs. Before anyone seeks God, he must recognize his need; and some appear never to have sensed their lost condition and the necessity of having their sins forgiven, but they are blind to spiritual light and are led by Satan.

Before the revival, from all appearances there seemed to be a general need on the campus. In the senior class were some who were not saved and would soon be leaving the school; consequently, the Holy Spirit impressed upon those who were praying, the urgency of the hour. A dullness and stupor had invaded the lives of even the Christians so that their testimonies were hindered and few souls sought God under their ministry. There were many who had certain needs that none save a merciful and and mighty God could meet.

Miss Lavetta Serrott, a member of the faculty, said that the students were not only at a low point spiritually, but the general conduct was such that it was not conducive to vital Christianity. She observed that there were many

"Testimonies were followed by confessions, by crowded altars, ... glorious spiritual victories, and this in turn ∞ more testimonies."

attitudes and feelings that were not befitting God's people. She relates that she was a little skeptical of the movement at first, but when she began to notice the lives that were changed and were dominated by a spirit of love and cooperativeness, her doubts of the genuineness of the revival soon faded.

There were even faculty members who had needs. As the Spirit moved, they became conscious of these and humbly knelt at the altar of prayer and in some cases meekly confessed they had harboured attitudes and feelings which were not Christian.

It is evident that the Spirit of God will reveal our needs and it is then our obligation to have them met, regardless of our position. When our needs are great we have a great God who is willing to meet them if we are willing to face these issues.

Don Gray, a student, in an article written for the Asbury Collegian, the campus newspaper, said:

> We here at Asbury had for sometime been shunning, belittling, and rebelling against the God that we so diligently serve. Our rebellion was not an open, declared warfare in most cases, but could more accurately be described as a silent, almost unwilling falling away from God. This process continued until many of us here were totally out of touch with God and yet professing to serve Him. There were students here bound by their sins and apparently satisfied to go ahead that way. Many who had trusted God for forgiveness of sins needed a purity and a power in their lives.
>
> The mere fact of our need was not enough to cause a revival to sweep down upon us. If this were true there would be thousands of places on earth more eligible for a revival than Asbury was, for our college is indeed a paradise if contrasted with other localities. We had many

needs but it wasn't until sincere people began recognizing these needs and becoming deeply concerned over them that there was any potential remedy.

The following was taken from the Christian Minister, by Dr. Mavis - April 1950:

This meeting is having a marvelous outreach. During the early days of the revival, telephone lines out of Wilmore were kept busy by students calling home to report their new found joys to their parents. Scores of students and others have gone to communities in Kentucky, Indiana, and Ohio and are helping spread the revival spirit. As this is being written (early in March), a great revival has been started in Mississippi. More than 200 people have sought God in one service there. Hundreds of people feel as one Seminary student said, "We are not being blessed of God to become spiritual ornaments, but to be used of Him." Scores of young people have been called into Christian service.

This meeting and others like it bring courage to evangelical Christians. Elements of the apostolic pattern have again been displayed. It indicates that men and women still recognize their need of God. It shows that the "power of God unto salvation" is applicable in the middle of the 20th century. It is a vivid proof that the days of revivals are not over and that they may be had when the conditions are met.

CHAPTER THREE
A Praying People

"And when they had prayed. . ."

THE FACT OF PRAYER

In the Asbury Alumnus of February, 1950, this article appeared:

> Some may be asking what is back of this revival? Perhaps there are several reasons which have combined to bring it about. One of these is the general spirit of revival which seems to be present in many sections where the people are willing to let God come on the scene as He did in the Graham revival in California, in the Wheaton revival, and in other places. Another and perhaps one of the most important factors is that it came in answer to earnest, persistent prayer. Some of the boys became deeply concerned about the unsaved of the school, particularly for several members of the senior class who had been here four years and were going out unsaved. They began to pray and others joined them. On the night before the revival broke out a group of boys had gathered in the gymnasium and prayed until after 2:00 o'clock in the morning, and other meetings were also being held in various rooms of the dormitories. Many testified during the meeting of their tremendous concern and their earnest prayer for God to come on the scene. This one factor more than any other, no doubt, is the real secret of the great outpouring of the Spirit which came upon the campus.

There remains little doubt in the minds of all who witnessed this mighty movement of the Holy Spirit that it was an answer to the fervent prayers of many people.

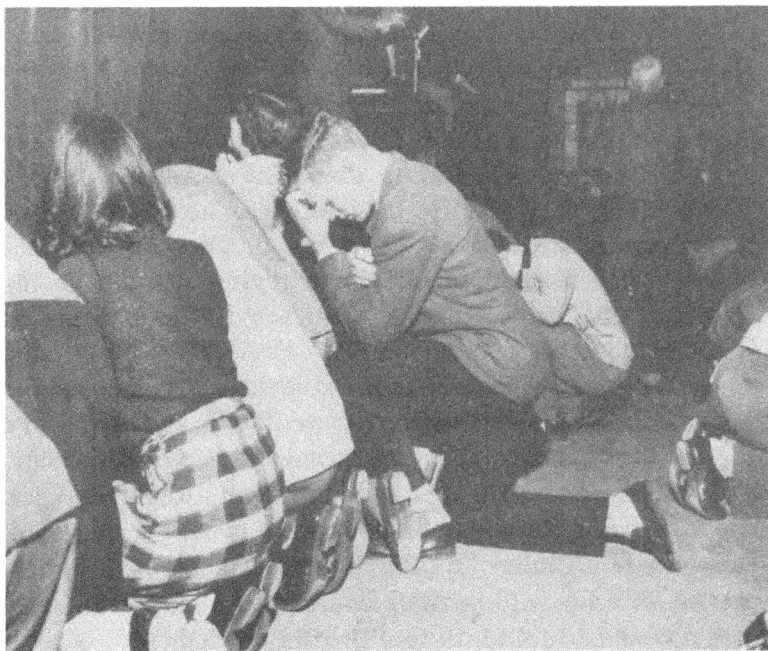

" Asbury has become an island of prayer . . . . "

Students and townspeople alike were praying for an outpouring of the Spirit upon the college and town. Groups were praying desperately for a refreshing visitation of God. It would be hard to point to any one person, or several persons or groups of persons and say that the revival came because of their prayers exclusively. However, the group which gathered in the gymnasium at the request of a student who was unsaved and his finding victory helped to start the revival at the chapel service the next morning as these boys began to testify.

Herbert Van Vorce was a student at Asbury College at this time. Apparently, "Herbie," as he was called by the students, needed spiritual help. The night before this revival started, Herbie was trying to study in his room at Morrison Cottage, but conviction became so great that study was impossible. He left his work, went downstairs, awakened a fellow student whom he asked to pray with him. The two boys went to a car and had a season of prayer, but they could not seem to pray through. Herbie suggested getting Bob Barefoot, whom he knew had been praying for months that he would make a full surrender to Christ. As they neared the dormitory, they met Bob, who said he was coming to hunt Herbie, because God had told him that Herbie needed help. So the three boys went to the old gymnasium and prayed until almost three in the morning, when the fire fell. In telling of this experience, Herbie said that when the Holy Spirit came, he felt as though dead and lay on the floor some time before being able to leave.

Herbie was used in a wonderful way by the Lord before he was called to be with the Saviour.

Here are some excerpts, received from Herbie's mother, taken from letters written by her son during this revival.

First letter:

It is Sunday again; I can truly say it has been one of the best Sundays in my life. Dwight Mik-

kelson and I with a few others went to Nicholas-
ville to the jail and had a service and then went
to Lexington and had a street meeting. We saw
a man about fifty years of age gloriously saved.
We went down in the slums for the service. How
ever, the man that was saved was a middle class
man whom we met uptown and gave a tract to.
. . . after talking a while he said he would like
to become a Christian. We went over to the
car and the man was gloriously saved.

Without doubt you have already sensed a change
in my life. Saturday morning at three o'clock
in the gym I settled it all with God. I started
praying at twelve and at about three o'clock the
fire fell. I put everything on the altar. Lois,
my life ambition, everything. I don't know, but
God has been revealing sermon after sermon to
me. It wouldn't surprise me if He had the ministry in mind for me. I am going ahead and continue trying to get in Med. School, trusting that
God's will will be worked out. I can say I never
have had such a glorious outpouring of the Holy
Spirit as I had the other night. God has been so
gracious to me by giving me Christian parents
who will take their stand for Jesus Christ and
the fullness of His Spirit.

I haven't had a good night's sleep for two weeks
until last night. Every night there would be a
text running through my mind. I don't feel like
a radical or that I am emotionally upset. I know
what I want and have settled it with God for time
and eternity.

Well, folks, I love you and I felt I should let
you know about my change and complete sub-
mission to God. Pray for me; I know that you
do without my asking.

Second letter:

How I wish you were here; it is wonderful what the Lord is doing. I have such peace and joy I can't express it. I can't write much because I have been in Heaven for three days, eaten three meals, had about three blessings, and walked about three hundred miles telling people that Jesus saves. I have asked, I don't know how many merchants in town to come and get right with God. It is an out-pouring of the Spirit. People are coming from all over, trying to figure it out and can't conceive of people shouting, getting to God. I am so glad I didn't wait for this to make my decision for Christ. I have victory like I never had before. God has laid His hand on me. I am burning up for Jesus; Praise His Name! Dad, I have got what you got; I have got it to stay. I am intoxicated with the Spirit; I can hardly write, my body feels like it is floating in heaven. I have finally caught hold of the hem of His garment. I am on the Gospel train that will stop at Hallelujah Station. I know you think I am going or gone crazy but God has so wonderfully got hold of me.

Reporters have been here from all over--you probably have heard about it. It is now headed for its seventieth hour without stopping (the revival.)

Between the second and third letters Herbie and some others had been in Mississippi holding meetings. The third letter was written at Wilmore.

Third letter:

God has marvellously helped me with my work; I am all caught up, ready to start studying for finals next week. If it is God's will, I am going back to Mississippi between quarters. We have no definite figure, but there were or have been

22

about two thousand seekers since we went to Mississippi. Dr. Anderson spoke in the Capitol building. We have no definite reports as yet on that service.

The Lord has so wonderfully blessed me I could never write in ink or explain in words what has been happening. I am going to the Church of the Open Door Sunday in Louisville. Pray much for this service. Then I have an invitation to go to North Carolina in the First Methodist Church in Durham for a week's meeting and a week-end meeting in Fort Valley, Georgia. I am anxious to see souls saved.

The revival in Mississippi is spreading throughout the state; we are getting calls in fifteen or twenty towns wanting some one to come for city-wide meetings. Oh, the power of God and how He can use us when we completely forget self and plunge in with God.

It all seems like a dream; I have been singing and testifying in huge churches and over radio stations that cover nine states, potentially thirty million people. It is unbelievable what God has done for me.

While in Mississippi I stayed in the home of Mrs. Osbourne; she is Marvin Osbourne's mother; he is on the campaign with us. It was Dr. Lindsey's radio station that we had access to. He also owns and operates the Mississippi Tabernacle, where we held the meetings. He was a wonderful help, and let the pastor and us boys take over the services.

Herbie was killed instantly by an electric shock on August 25, 1951, in Findlay, Ohio, while engaged in construction work. One of his last messages to his family was: "If you ever get a telegram saying I have gone unexpectedly, don't worry. I will be WITH JESUS." It is estimated that several hundred persons found Christ during a brief year and a half as a result of Herb's glowing testimony in meetings in which he assisted in Mississippi, Texas, New York, and Kentucky. Now he has been called to a higher ministry.

At the funeral service, in Wilmore, Kentucky, Chaplain Van Vorce asked to give his son's testimony. Vividly he recalled events leading up to Herb's remarkable conversion, preceding Asbury's spontaneous revival. Herb phoned his folks, then in Texas: "Dad, I have good news for you and Mom. At three o'clock this morning in the old Gymn I said: 'Lord, you can have my life, my all, for the ministry or the mission field or whatever you want.'" A week later he phoned again: "Dad, you must come to Wilmore! The greatest revival I have ever seen is here. I did not know it could be so wonderful. We have left this world and have gone to another."

Chaplain and Mrs. Van Vorce had the joy of visiting Lois and Herb one week before the accident.

"I do not question the love of God," the father said. "I am going back to camp with a new determination to preach the love of God and His power to sustain through the darkest hours! . . . God's will is our will. My hope and prayer is that the mantle of this life might fall on some other boy or boys that they may go forth to do even greater things than 'Herbie' could have done."

FERVENT PRAYER

Prayer was thought by many to be one of the most important factors contributing to the power of the revival. God honored the prayers of persons whose names will never be connected with this movement. Many obscure Christians had poured out their souls to God in the secret of their homes or rooms not only at Asbury College and in Wilmore, but over the world.

Through the years there have been those far from Asbury who have prayed continually not only for Asbury

College, but for her sister institution, Asbury Seminary. Some on beds of affliction were not able to do anything but pray. These faithful prayer warriors are aware of the important job these institutions have of training young people, who are making decisions as to how they will invest their lives in the years that lie ahead. They sense the importance of building character and instilling convictions in the lives of these who will be leaders in the various religious fields around the world. There is a desperate need for a "spirit-filled ministry" today. If the standard which Christ set is to be upheld, we must have this type of ministry; otherwise there will be a decline in the moral lives of our country. Prayer is the answer to this problem!

This article was written by Dr. W. C. Mavis, Head of Pastoral Work at Asbury Theological Seminary. This was taken from the Christian Minister, issued April, 1950:

> For several weeks before the meeting started there had been much earnest prayer for an outpouring of the Spirit of God. Groups of students and faculty people met in the dormitory rooms, class rooms, and offices to pray. This spirit of prayer continued while the meeting was in progress. Frequently every room in the college auditorium building was occupied by groups of people in silent prayer. At other times, as the main service was in progress, the voices of prayer could be heard in other parts of the building. One reporter remarked, "Asbury has become an island of prayer."

During the revival there were prayer meetings in progress everywhere, in the dormitories, in the classrooms, in the dining hall, in the gymnasium, on the campus, and in the homes of Wilmore residents. A spirit of prayer seemed to possess each person that had attended the services and felt the presence of God. It was common to hear the praying of Christians from almost any point of the campus. They offered petitions first for themselves that they might be used of God without hindrance and then that sinners might be saved through their witness.

These people whose lives were revitalized were now in a condition to pray for the lost, not only in Wilmore, but in the surrounding towns and communities. It was not until then that students could really pray for their classmates. Now the Christian people had a burden for the lost people of the world. Fellow-students who were not saved recognized the difference in the lives of Christian students which became a definite witness. When Christians let the Holy Spirit search their hearts, allow Him to meet their spiritual needs, and want their lives to be in the center of the will of God, He can use them to win souls. Again, prayer is the answer!

Dean Kenyon, writing for the Asbury Collegian, said:

Some of the best revivals that Asbury College has ever had have been those that broke out spontaneously among the students. The present revival is very much like some of those we had in the earlier days when a group of students got together and through prayer a revival began. For some time on the campus there had been considerable praying among groups; . . . the spirit of a revival was being created, and there was no question that a great refreshing was the result.

There was a general need felt on our campus for this outpouring of the Holy Spirit, which was truly an answer to prayer. Many confessions were made, many restitutions took place, and it has been a great uplift to faculty and students, as well as friends in the community.

Ruby Vahey, writing for the Asbury Collegian says this concerning the prayer life of the campus:

Early Friday morning, shortly after dawn, several hundred students returned to the auditorium and knelt and prayed. It was 'World Day of Prayer' and their requests encompassed the globe. Classes were resumed at eight o'clock, but those who were free at that hour found it impossible to tear themselves away from the sacred spot. Teachers and students were unable to bring themselves back so suddenly from the heavenly to the earthly, and every class that morning was transformed into a prayer or praise meeting.

Not only did prayer change things at Asbury, but it was an encouragement to other churches and communities to believe God for an outpouring of His Holy Spirit. Many were attracted to this place of prayer.

If these conditions could be met in every phase of Christian endeavor - in the pastorates, in the evangelistic field, and on the mission fields of the world, the work would take on a new meaning. Men and women would become so hungry for salvation that nothing could stop them from being completely satisfied!

This article was taken from the Dallas Morning News, February 25. (UP):

A religious revival that made Asbury College an island of prayer is attracting persons from other Kentucky cities to this small town.

There was no indication early this morning as to when the prayers and testimonials would end. About 300 persons remained in Hughes Auditorium despite the pleas from college authorities that the meeting be discontinued until morning.

Since 9:00 a.m. Thursday, services have been held continuously. Students and townspeople have crowded the altar, prayed for forgiveness and professed their faith.

Jack Lewyn, reporter for the Herald-Leader, stated:

Prayer, and little else, dominated life in this little Jessamine County college tonight.

Voices toned with sincerity and eyes sparkling with a dampness of inner realization were uplifted to God as a thousand revival participants prayed and rendered testimonies with undiminishing dedication.

A general revival session in Hughes Memorial Auditorium on the Asbury College campus was suspended temporarily shortly after noon, but as an overcast sky faded into nightfall, the 1,200-capacity chapel, almost large enough to accomodate the town's population, echoed again with declarations of faith.

The suspension followed a morning-long series of faculty testimonies and prayers, but the revival has never been interrupted since it began at 9:00 a.m. Thursday when a student stood and asked to make a testimony.

Although the chapel was closed for an hour, groups of 50 or more students and townspeople continued to pray and 'find God' in meetings in dormitories, homes and other campus chapels.

Dr. Johnson said it was urgent that the revival continue. He told Dr. Kenyon he would fly home from Florida tonight or Sunday.

Shortly after Hughes Auditorium was reopened, the participants began returning in small groups to pray, confess, and testify perhaps throughout the night amid patient, impressive meditation.

"The end is not yet," said Dr. James Robertson, professor at Asbury Theological Seminary, who spoke at the usual chapel period.

Despite the shouts, the declarations, individual and grouped, an air of meditation prevailed as students, older folks and children knelt with heads bowed and eyes damp. Many never shouted, but prayed silently with a depth of feeling.

When the hymns resounded, the singing became almost thunderous. It is doubtful that any participant has been active continually since the session began as an every-day chapel meeting, but the fervor became so apparent today that school officials thought a rest should be ordered.

This service rolled on through the night with some sixty sleepy students remaining in the auditorium kneeling in prayer. Others returned to dormitories to get some rest, but many, instead of sleeping, held prayer meetings in rooms.

These meetings proved that when people want a revival and are willing to pay the price for it, God will not disappoint them. In many cases those who prayed found peace and went to fellow-students to make restitution for wrongs done. This procedure paved the way for those to whom the restitution was made to began to investigate their own spiritual lives.

THE RESULT OF PRAYER

Anyone attending the services will affirm that there was little or no criticism of others. This was a time of self-examination and not a time for finding faults in the lives of others. Denominational differences were forgotten, all the people were as one, and Jesus was exalted, as on the day of Pentecost.

Some interesting incidents connected with the revival were recounted in Dr. Holland's article of March 15 in the Pentecostal Herald:

Sunday night two young men came from the Baptist College at Campbellsville, Kentucky.

They were so blessed that they drove home seventy miles after service and brought back between twenty and thirty of their fellow-students, arriving at Wilmore at four o'clock Monday morning, while the service of prayer and praise was still on. The students felt the need of help, and sent for Dr. Anderson, a faculty member, to come to their aid. He came, preached to them for thirty minutes and had an altar call; with the result that many were blessed. They left at five-thirty o'clock, in time to get home for school; but they returned on Monday evening with a larger delegation

A freshman was wonderfully sanctified. He felt he must tell his mother and help her into the Christian experience. He secured an auto and drove two hundred miles to his home in Tennessee. He told the good news to his mother and brought her back with him in time for her to be gloriously saved in the service that evening.

A Salvation Army captain from Middletown, Ohio, on his way to a week-end engagement, turned on his radio and got the news report of the revival. He turned in this direction. After filling his engagement on Sunday, he was back again On Monday.

We made no complete record of visitors, but we know people came from Michigan, Illinois, Indiana, Ohio, Tennessee, West Virginia, Florida, Mississippi, Georgia, and from all over Kentucky.

After a spontaneous desire to call his home at Brookhaven, Mississippi, a student asked her two unsaved brothers to come for the revival. One brother was a soldier who was home on furlough after having just returned from Okinawa. Both accepted their sister's invitation, and, with their mother, drove a distance of seven hundred miles, arriving at Asbury at 8:30 p.m. Sunday evening. Shortly after entering Hughes Auditorium, they responded to the exhortation, given by Dr. T. M. Anderson, and made their way to the already-filled altar, where they were gloriously saved. The following evening one of the brothers felt his need for the baptism of the Holy Spirit and was sanctified. The Christian mother rejoiced exceedingly over the two victories for which she had been praying for years. The members of the family group were thankful that they had driven such a great distance to share in the blessing of the revival.

A student was riding south on a bus and fell into conversation with a preacher just behind the driver. The bus driver, hearing what they said about the revival, became so convicted that he requested permission of the passengers to pull to the side of the road for a period of prayer.

These experiences were taken from the Asbury Collegian of March 4, 1950 (Revival Edition).

One of the far-reaching aspects of the present college revival is that of the spiritual vision and evangelistic zeal received by many visitors who have come to the Asbury campus during these days of richest blessing. Many are returning to their respective homes and localities, having received definite experiences of salvation and sanctification, with a sincere desire to share their newly-found victories with friends and loved ones.

At 2:00 a.m. Monday, a call was received from a student at Kentucky Wesleyan College, who asked whether the revival was continuing. Several students arrived later that morning from the college to receive inspiration from the services, and they returned with a desire to share the revival spirit with their fellow students.

During Sunday night's service a group of twenty-five local high school students came forward to testify of God's saving grace. Two Wilmore high school girls said that they hoped to start a prayer meeting in their school on Monday during the lunch hour.

A seventeen-year-old high school student said that he had come from his home in Irving, Kentucky, about fifty miles away. He stated that he had received a real experience and wanted to take it home to his school and community. A Lexington high school student also testified that he had a desire to take the spirit of the revival home and share it with others.

A student from the Southern Baptist Theological Seminary, Louisville, said with deepest sincerity, "My prayer is that I may carry back with me something just like this, along with the power that is here."

A youth group of the Calvary Holiness Church arrived on campus Saturday for the revival service. One grade school student who was present, witnessed in his church on the following day and requested prayer for his schoolmates.

Not to be excluded from the number who traveled miles to participate in the revival was our own college president, Dr. Z. T. Johnson, who journeyed a distance of 920 miles from Lakeland, Florida.

No doubt many traveled great distances who have not been mentioned.

In his book Prevailing Prayer Dr. Anderson gives an interesting incident about prayer in connection with the Asbury Revival:

There was a young woman who was unmoved by the power of God manifested in the great revival at Asbury College, in 1950. She told some of the students that it was nothing but emotionalism and excitement and that she would have nothing to do with it. Several students requested me to join them in prayer for the girl to be saved. About four o'clock in the morning I presented this girl before the throne of grace. I did not know the young woman, but the moment I began to pray for her, I saw her running out of a lighted building and running toward the darkness. The vision so impressed me that I told some of the students to inform the young woman that I had seen her running from God.

About nine thirty that night, the young woman came to my home. She sat on a small footstool in front of me, and in anger told me that she wanted no part of the revival, that it was all emotionalism and religious excitement. I could not reason with her, for she was very angry at me for sending word to her about running from God.

In my own mind, I was convinced that her attitude toward the revival was a pretense and that her real reason was covering her sins. I told her I could find her real reason for rejecting the Saviour, and I began to pray for her. When I presented her before the Saviour, I saw a large hall, and an orchestra and the leader of the orchestra standing before a microphone. But my attention was drawn to a young man playing the piano; I knew he had something to do with this girl's attitude toward Christ. When I asked the girl about the young man, she began to cry; and confessed that she had been attending the dance and was at one time planning to marry the piano player. She said it was a secret and was amazed that I knew it.

As I began to pray again for her, I saw a lighted room and a table set; and this young woman filling the glasses with liquor. When I asked her if she drank liquor, she began to scream and said, "That is a cocktail party given in my home, and I gave a preacher's daughter her first drink. I have damned her; I have damned my best friend." She confessed covering her many evil deeds by pretending that she did not believe in the revival. She had no more fight against conviction left in her; she was completely broken in spirit, and was contrite of heart. Once more I took her to the Saviour in prayer and I obtained mercy for her at the throne of grace. The merciful Lord saved her instantly; and she shouted with great joy for deliverance from sin.

"For three days there was never a time when there were not people waiting in line to give testimonies."

CHAPTER FOUR

A Spirit-filled People

" . . . the place was shaken where they were assembled together; and they were all filled with the Holy Ghost."

THE FACT OF SPIRIT-FILLED PEOPLE

Those who attended the revival can never forget how the meetings were all led by the Holy Ghost. Dr. Holland in one of his articles remarked:

> An interesting feature about these meetings is the fact that the Holy Spirit is the leader. Preachers and preaching are not in prominence. God leads, the people obey, and great are the results. Dr. T. M. Anderson, a member of the faculty, did give an occasional exhortation. It is glorious to see the leadership of the Spirit.

The Asbury Alumnus of January 1950 had this to say:

One of the distinctive features of the present revival at Asbury is that it has been marked by a minimum of emphasis on the element of human leadership and direction, particularly in its early stages. There were no preaching services as such but a stream of testimonies, confessions, and seekers at the altar. On the first morning of the outbreak students began to run to the altar almost at the beginning of the testimonies and there was an almost continuous stream of seekers for five days and nights as the tide seemed to rise with the passing of time in spite of the weariness and physical fatigue as students, townspeople, faculty and visitors sought the Lord for the needs of their hearts. As news of the revival spread through the press, over the radio, and by personal contacts, visitors began to pour in from near and far. Some who came out of mere curiosity at first later sought the Lord for their own needs. Friends and relatives, some of them from several hundred miles away, came and a number were graciously saved or received a new touch of God on their lives and then added their testimony to those of the others. As the revival progressed three persons, Dean J. B. Kenyon, Dr. W. W. Holland, and Dr. T. M. Anderson, came more and more to be projected into the position of providing the little human leadership which was needed; but the remarkable thing about the whole meeting was the way in which the Holy Spirit seemed to deal directly with individual hearts, without any preaching, with very little exhortation, and with little more than a brief invitation, seekers knelt at the altar to find spiritual help and victory.

Another remarkable aspect of the revival was the spirit of honesty, sincerity, genuineness, and the willingness to follow the leadership of the Spirit. Many rose to confess their failures and sins publicly, many went to those they had wronged or criticized to apologize and ask forgiveness, and others made restitution of wrong doing as the Holy Spirit brought the matter to their attention. The result was to produce such a beautiful sense of love and harmony among all that we felt we were moving in an atmosphere that was indeed heavenly.

There are certain facts about the revival that were probably never realized by many of those who were there at each service. Truly, all who participated will affirm that they were impressed with the wondrous spirit that prevailed.

However, even with this atmosphere that appeared

"It was a marvellous sight to see hundreds of hands spontaneously raised

in personal affirmation as the great hymns of the church were sung."

almost heavenly there were problems and difficulties which presented themselves at times. Satan certainly throws all his forces into action when there comes a time of refreshing like this. At these times he tries hard to discourage and defeat.

Dean Kenyon asserts that if it had not been for the volume of prayer that went up he would have faltered under the load which was unexpectedly cast upon him. Many phone calls from townspeople gave encouragement and strength for the great task. At times he hardly knew which way to turn, but through much prayer and faith he was able to lead the school until Dr. Johnson returned.

Situations arose, about which the general public will never know. Here are a few problems, which will give the reader an idea of the circumstances.

The stage in Hughes Auditorium was set up with curtains hanging ready for a dress rehearsal scheduled for Thursday night of the day the revival began. The praying and testimonials continued throughout the day and increased in momentum.

Those in charge of producing the play were at a loss as to what to do. It was felt that continuing with it as planned would be detrimental to the success of the revival. Finally, it was decided that the play should be postponed indefinitely.

The play was to supply the Junior Class with money for their project of moving and restoring the original Asbury building. To make up, at least in part, the sum which the class expected to receive from the production, Dean Kenyon decided to have a special offering. From it about two hundred dollars was cleared for the project. The leading of the Spirit in each circumstance was wondrous to behold.

Then came the problem of the unexpected publicity. When those in charge heard about the news items, they began to wonder exactly what to do. They were afraid the publicity would be detrimental to the revival. They did not want to risk it.

However, newsmen were there the very first night and their cameras flashed intermittently throughout the service; but such was the Divine Presence that no one seemed to notice them. The Louisville and the Lexington papers gave the news release, which spread rapidly throughout the nation.

There was much publicity given to the revival in the press and radio. Portions were televised. For a number of days the Asbury revival as a news feature ranked second only to the steel strike which was on at that time.

On February 26, eight persons, representing the United Press, the Associated Press, and the Television of NBC, came upon the campus and remained for eight hours. Mr. Jordan of radio station WVLK called and asked the privilege of broadcasting the service over his station.

Dean Kenyon had nothing but praise for the newsmen for the excellent way in which they presented their stories to the public. "We here at the college, including our students," he told them, "have been most pleased with the manner in which you people have conducted yourselves while here and the way in which pictures and stories have been handled. We feel that the good publicity you have given us should be continued if you see fit, because it will serve to show folk here in Kentucky and in other states that we are sincere about this revival and its sole purpose, which is to bring people back to God."

Along with the activities of the revival, there was the responsibility of maintaining the normal operation of the college. While Dr. Johnson was in a meeting in Florida, Dean Kenyon was contacting him each day, trying to relate to him the occurences on the campus, seeking to be advised by the president and to be guided by the Holy Spirit.

Dr. Johnson was of the opinion that the revival was needed; therefore, each day he encouraged Dean Kenyon to carry on as long as the Spirit led in the services.

Many phone calls came to the office of Dean Kenyon. Dr. Johnson and the Dean received numerous letters from all over the country, from Massachusetts to Hollywood, California, containing thanks to God for his visitation, and requests for prayer for revivals in the writers' churches. Many were asking for gospel teams to come and assist in meetings in various communities.

Some who were not present may say that the revival was too emotional. However, those who attended these services and saw the leadership of the Holy Spirit will affirm that there was order at all times. There were many "Amens" and "Hallelujahs" when the testimonies were given. At times there was shouting, but this blended into the service and many times was hardly noticed. There was liberty here.

This interesting account written by John Gibson, was taken from the Courier-Journal, Louisville, Kentucky.

Voices of the hundreds gathered in the 1,200 seat auditorium resounded throughout the chapel and drifted through the open windows as hymns were sung. Most of the seats were occupied and many persons were standing at the rear of the chapel.

The hundreds rose to their feet, stretching their arms toward the heavens, as one song followed another. Many left their chapel seats to pray at the altar, so crowded that others knelt and buried their heads in their hands at the front row of seats.

The display of religious fervor, orderly at all times, was spontaneous.

Dr. J. B. Kenyon, dean of the school, termed the movement the "most genuine revival the school has had in some time."

"We have no apologies to make," Kenyon said over the loudspeaking system. "We have found our God anew." A great murmur of assent rose from the lips of the gathered worshippers to greet this statement.

"We may, at times, make a lot of noise," the dean continued, "but don't let that bother you. I've heard a lot more noise at a ball game when the batter strikes out. And isn't this the biggest home run of them all"?

"I've been asked when this will stop. I have only this to say that as long as the Spirit moves you, we have no intention of halting your testimonies."

The following article was taken from the Christian Advocate of March 16, 1950:

Shortly after Wheaton College students were moved to a testimony marathon, fervor gripped independent Methodist Asbury College in Wilmore, Kentucky, where a spontaneous revival began on Thursday, February 23, and lasted until Tuesday, when classes were resumed but with a nightly revival added.

Hughes Memorial Auditorium, which seats 1,200, overflowed frequently. President Z. T. Johnson wired, "Testimonials, prayers, exhortations, altar calls. Movings of the Spirit penetrating and widespread. Most genuine revival I have ever witnessed. Hundreds of visitors. Numerous college and university visitors converted and sanctified. Affecting whole neighborhood."

All recognized the compulsion of the Holy Spirit and felt the unmistakably sense of divine presense in all the services. Dr. Robertson, a member of the Seminary faculty said it was an "unusual visitation of God!"

From the Asbury Alumnus, January 1950, the following was selected:

As one reporter in a newspaper in Lexington, Kentucky, put it, the attempt to describe or record the scene defies the best efforts of the press or camera. Perhaps the experience of the early disciples when the Holy Spirit descended upon them on the day of Pentecost is more nearly akin to it than anything else that may be likened to it. There was a definite sense of the presence of the glory and the power of God like the disciples must have felt on the mount of transfiguration or like that which came to Isaiah when he saw the Lord high and lifted up and His glory filling the temple.

Another unusual feature of the revival was the encouragement to other groups to pray and believe God for a refreshing with the result that reports came in from other communities of victories they had received. Some came to see and experience the refreshing of the Lord at Asbury and then went back to their communities to kindle a new flame of revival fire on the altars of their own churches or in their communities. Groups came from other colleges to see; then went back to their schools to carry the spirit there. It was not long before doors began to open and calls began to come in for groups to go to churches of various communities to help them start a revival there.

In a recent report of services held by various groups it was estimated that some four thousand or more had received definite victory as a result of the revival at the college and various places where groups had gone out to other communities.

THE RESULT OF BEING SPIRIT-FILLED

The result of spirit-filled lives was tremendous. There came unusual opportunities to witness. The Spirit would use mere testimonies in many services, and people would be convicted and find victory at the altars.

Dr. Robert Coleman, a student at the Seminary at that time, and now professor of Evangelism at the Seminary, said he went to his church that weekend of the revival but had no preaching service. Testimonies were given and seven people were at the altar at the end of the service.

The following accounts of experiences were taken from Dr. Holland's article in the Pentecostal Herald:

Rev. R. E. Case, pastor of the Wells Memorial Methodist Church of Jackson, Mississippi, called by phone, requesting that a gospel team be sent to help him in a revival. A kind lady paid their transportation by air, and two students from Asbury College and one from Asbury Theological Seminary were on their way within a short time. They phoned back the next day, stating that the church was packed and people were standing in the streets, and between fifty and sixty people were at the altar. The next day, they were invited to move to the largest tabernacle in the city of Jackson, with all of the facilities at their command.

Here is the story of that meeting as told by the pastor himself:

Four students came by plane from Asbury to give a report on the great outpouring of the Holy Spirit there during the spontaneous revival in February, 1950. I was the pastor of Wells, and two of the students who came in that group were members of our church. We had a few spot announcements on the radio that the students were

45

coming. They arrived late Wednesday afternoon by plane and came directly to the church. I was impressed with the holy hush and quietness that seemed to exist among these four students. They went into a room in the rear of the church for a period of prayer. I went out into the foyer of the church to greet the people who were beginning to arrive. This same holy hush seemed to prevail as the people gathered into the sanctuary. No one talked above a whisper. Some of our people went to the altar and prayed silently.

The service began at 7:30 o'clock. It consisted of singing, testifying, and exhortation. Each member of the group told about the revival at Asbury and of the tremendous blessing they had received. Each one of them closed his testimony with a plea for the people of the audience to receive Christ as their Saviour and Sanctifier. The altar was filled twice that evening. The power of God was felt mightily. It was around ten o'clock, as I remember, when the service was over. We announced a service on the following night.

Thursday and Friday nights were almost duplicates of Wednesday night except that the people of the congregation joined in the testimonies. God was present, and His power could be felt in an unusual way. On Saturday afternoon, Dr. T. M. Anderson arrived by plane with four more Asbury students. Saturday night was a high spot in the revival for us all. There were perhaps a dozen preachers on the rostrum. Dr. Anderson was the master of ceremonies, but at times one of the young preachers was in charge. "Amazing Grace" was sung in the spirit, and tears flowed while shouts of praise went up. Preachers embraced each other on the rostrum, and the people wept. Dr. Anderson brought a message, and the altar was lined with seekers.

Sunday was a high day, especially Sunday evening. The revival went on for twenty-eight nights. Dr. Anderson preached each evening for about two weeks. During the day, groups would visit schools and colleges, and each day there were radio messages, testimonies, and reports of the revival.

More Asbury boys came. Some went to Hattiesburg, Mississippi, to Broadstreet Church, of which Rev. Andrew Gallman was pastor, and a revival broke out there. Another group started a revival at Natchez, Mississippi. Everything was informal. Speakers spoke extemporaneously. Men would come down the aisle and upon the rostrum to testify and exhort.

The boys from Asbury, as well as Dr. Anderson, stressed the fulness of the Spirit. Visitors, who had never heard the doctrine preached, were impressed, and before long they were at the altar seeking the experience.

I remember one lady who came. She had a very pleasant personality, and the people were deeply impressed with her testimony. No one could doubt that she was a saved person. One night, as we were leaving the church, this lady said to me, "Brother Case, this is wonderful. I know that I am saved, but I do not have what these young men are preaching, the Baptism with the Holy Spirit. Do you have any books that you could let me read on the doctrine?" I assured her that I did, and that I would bring them to her the next night. This lady told me a couple of nights later that she was "simply revelling in these books," especially Wood's Perfect Love. She was sanctified in her home. She called us and told us about it. She was weeping over the phone. I gave her a special opportunity to testify to the experience before the whole congregation. She had a Calvinist background, but this did not stand in the way of her receiving the experience.

People came to the revival from six states. Of course, we could not accomodate the crowds. We had all night prayer meetings. Services lasted as late as two and three o'clock in the morning. It was a time of refreshing from the Lord.

A noteworthy fact about this revival was the absence of denominational lines. The Holy Spirit prevailed, and a spirit of love was there. Each service saw the sanctuary filled to overflowing. God was there. Prayer went up almost constantly. We experienced a foretaste of heaven.

I have found people from time to time who were saved in that revival. It seemed that more people outside of our church were blessed in a definite manner than were those of our membership. It was truly a wonderful visitation of God among us. We thank Him for permitting us to have the experience.

Another student felt called to drive to Mt. Carmel, some ninety miles from Wilmore, and hold a meeting. He went and returned Monday morning in time to meet the Campbellsville group and reported twenty-two persons wonderfully sanctified in the meeting.

The president of the student body left late Thursday night for his home in Kimball, West Virginia, to start a revival. When he returned he reported that he left it going at a high speed. He felt that the four hundred mile drive was more than worthwhile.

A trio of three young ladies, one of whom had drifted from God, sang in the meeting. One testified before they sang. The other two were asked to testify after the song. One of them did, but the other said that she needed God and requested prayer. She fell at the altar and prayed through to victory.

From the Asbury Collegian of March 4, 1950, (Revival Edition) comes these reports:

The present spiritual revival while centering in Hughes Auditorium on the campus of the college, was participated in quite fully by both students and faculty of the Seminary. Classes were dismissed whenever possible, giving to Seminary people the privilege of attending the meetings. Students and faculty attended as a group at the chapel hour on Tuesday. Seminarians have been very much in evidence in the evening services.

The outpouring of the Holy Spirit in these days has resulted in great blessing to many Seminary students. Many who have had unsettled spiritual problems found new joy and peace as the Spirit of God had His way in their hearts and lives. Some entered into the sanctified life.

The Seminary family rejoices with the college in the gracious blessings of these days.

The Messengers of the Lord quartet went out this past week-end to share their cups of blessings with those who were thirsting after righteousness. The Holy Spirit is dealing in a special way with hearts all over the United States.

God blessed Ford Philpot's messages with twenty seekers at Mt. Carmel Church Saturday evening, and there were approximately thirty seekers at Epworth Methodist Church In Lexington Sunday evening.

After testimonies began at Little Texas Mission, the planned sermon had to be put aside. In both the morning and evening services souls found satisfaction in their Lord Jesus.

Hearts melted and tears flowed freely down the cheeks of many at Ludlow Methodist Church in Ludlow, Kentucky, as God blessed the testimonies and songs of five students from Asbury. There were five victories plus many requests for prayer.

Earl Bishop, student, and his group held services in saloons as well as in the church. Hearts were touched. Truth always is victorious.

Twelve at Fort Valley, Georgia, found God after listening to the testimonies and prayers of another group of Asburians.

Fifteen young people knelt at the altar in Corbin, Kentucky, searching for soul satisfaction. George Rose and Phil Peace, under the direction of our Lord, were in charge.

Jesus visited the prison at Frankfort, Kentucky, and freed two souls. Then another found the Lord at a meeting there.

At the Salvation Army Post in Danville nine persons joined the forces of truth.

Janie Kunkel, Marilyn Loy, and Beverly Sund were thrilled to the depths of their souls when they saw God's Holy Spirit move the hearts of the people in the churches of Lanesville, Indiana, and New Middletown, Indiana. Shouts and sobs were heard and heart wringings were felt as testimonies were given. It had been a long time since such emotions were displayed in the churches.

At the time of the revival at Asbury, one of the students, Wayne Patton, was youth director at the Hiland Methodist Church in Fort Thomas, Kentucky. He called from Asbury asking his parents to tell the young people that a wonderful revival had broken out at the college and to invite them to come down if they could.

Two young men, Don Walsh and Bill Parker, who had been saved in a week-end revival that was held by Wayne and Bob Scott at Fort Thomas came and both through the ministry of Dr. T. M. Anderson were sanctified wholly.

They went back to northern Kentucky and a few days after that were in a sub-district meeting in one of the churches in that area. The Lord so mightily moved on the group through these testimonies these young men gave that the minister in charge felt compelled to give an altar call at once. About forty young people sought the Lord. There was such joy among the converts that those in charge thought that they ought to do something to keep the fires burning. So they began Saturday night evangelistic services under the name of The Christian Youth of Northern Kentucky. Wayne was put in charge of directing the meetings. He would plan for the music and preachers for the Saturday night services.

This organization continued for four years and many revivals, prayer meetings, and Bible studies were sponsored by this group of young people. The impact was felt all over northern Kentucky. A number of young people, some of whom are here now, came to Asbury College as a result.

These meetings attracted youth from 15 and 20 miles away. During the first year the altar services were very seldom barren. The pastors supported these services very well.

Those from other denominations began to attend the services also. One night a Catholic girl was saved and this was a glorious time indeed.

Other manifestations of the Spirit were seen at Versailles, St. Louis, Missouri, and at Woodland Heights Mission. Souls were saved and hearts were purified. Many requested prayer.

There were probably numbers of similar incidents which have not been recorded.

CHAPTER FIVE
A Witnessing People

" . . . and they spake the word of God with boldness."

VICTORIOUS WITNESSING AND HEARTY SINGING

The following paragraph, taken from an article in the Christian Minister, was written by Dr. Mavis;

> This was not a preaching meeting as have been most of the revivals during the 20th century. No sermon was delivered until the evening of the fourth day. Victorious witnessing was a prominent feature of the meeting. Hundreds of people, most of them young, gave testimonies of having been saved, sanctified, or having received some other definite spiritual victory. These testimonies were radiant, natural, and definite, and stereotyped testimonies were the exception. The public 'confession' element was at a minimum though many private confessions and restitutions were made. The writer heard scores of testimonies and not one contained objectionable elements. The press reporters who visited this meeting were deeply impressed with the reports of victory. Some of them quietly walked about as if they were on holy ground. After one college girl had witnessed to her personal commitment to God, one reporter, evidently unaccustomed to personal witnessing, stated that it seemed an·intrusion to be present.

> Especially during the early stages of this meeting the singing was spontaneous and thrilling. It was a marvellous sight to see hundreds of hands spontaneously and sincerely raised in personal affirmation as the great hymns of the church were sung. Little attention was given to the lighter religious songs. "Amazaing Grace"

"These testimonies were radiant, natural, and definite .... "

was sung more than any other hymn. The writer noted that during one two-hour period this hymn was spontaneously repeated four times. Other hymns that were sung over and over were "There is a Fountain Filled with Blood" and "What Can Wash Away My Sin?"

The use of the great hymns was one of the indications that this was not just a religious pep meeting. It did not resemble an enthusiastic get-together wherein zealous collegians cheered "Hurrah for Jesus." One could not attend for even an hour, without recognizing the presence of the Spirit in a most profound manner. When the writer first attended, he immediately noted people kneeling alone in prayer everywhere in the auditorium; others sat quietly weeping or remained quiet as the Spirit dealt with them, and still others gave their testimonies.

Jack Lewyn, of the Lexington Leader staff had this report to give February 25, 1950:

A co-ed at the interdenominational school, walked to a rostrum on the chapel stage and shouted: "Praise the Lord. . . because He met my need . . . I've never felt like this before; I never knew the glory of Christ.

During each pronunciation, shouts of "Hallelujah" rang throughout the auditorium, affirming convictions.

Many confessed having found fault with their brethren and asked forgiveness. Others spoke firmly of their faith in God the Almighty.

During tonight's service, one man stood and testified:

"I said I've been a Christian for nine years. I've been lying to you." He said he had not, until now, been complete in his faith.

Dr. C. B. Hamann, a college professor, said he would like to see the old Methodist tradition of class meetings adopted.

He asked two men, one elderly and one middle-aged, to testify to their experiences -- and they did.

A wave of testimonies subsided, then rose again after a period of quiet reverent meditation.

Dr. T. M. Anderson, teacher in the Department of Bible, takes the rostrum and there is an altar call. Students come down the aisles singing, to join their fellows in prayer. Then more testimonials, many from students who are coming to the platform. During the lunch-time lull, that part of the audience remaining in the chapel kneels in prayer, at their seats or at the altar.

These following testimonies were taken from the Lexington Leader printed February 25, 1950.

A spontaneous marathon religious revival rolled into the third continuous day at Asbury College to the accompaniment of hymns and tearful testimonies.

Townspeople and faculty members stood a little in awe of what Dean J. B. Kenyon called "a sincere demonstration of faith," as hundreds of students lined up to "testify for God."

A blind student said he hoped "the revival would spread to the state university at Lexington."

Each student who was to speak walked to the front of a velvet curtain drawn before a stage set for the play, "Our Hearts Were Young and Gay." The play, scheduled to be given Friday night and tonight by the Junior class, was postponed indefinitely.

Another student, an ex-member of the German Army and former prisoner of war in this country, said, "It certainly is strange that I, a German who fought against the Americans, could come to a school like Asbury and make so many hundreds of friends.

"It all goes to show that God is everywhere," he added. "The only way for unity is through God."

Men and women students alike wept openly as their classmates unburdened themselves, told how troubled their hearts had been and how happy they were to have confessed their faith openly.

"My heart was sad until I met Jesus," one girl said.

A Korean student, full of emotion but at a loss for words, said, "My tongue will not work but I have a big heart."

Several students told the audience of some 1,200 that their parents still were living in sin. About a dozen said they had come to the predominantly religious school more or less over the objections of their parents, and were discouraged from talking about religious subjects at home.

In the Courier-Journal of February 27, 1950, these testimonies were reported by Joe Reister, a staff correspondent:

"I came from an un-Christian home and I had to find Christ on my own. I found Him here at Asbury and now I'm convinced that God is far above everything else."

"I wish my dear mother were here. I love the Lord with all my heart," Mike Jordan, student from Hattiesburg, Mississippi.

Jordan later told a photographer for the Courier-Journal, who made his picture while he was testifying:

"That flash bulb popping reminded me of the light that has poured onto my soul during this revival."

Many of the students admit they are almost ready to drop from physical exhaustion. But they said they are still spiritually strong.

"I'm awfully tired, physically," one co-ed sighed, "but I'm not the least bit tired spiritually."

An 80-year-old man told of finding God anew.

The testimonies of many participants were almost inaudible at times when the group shouted affirmations.

Another student stood and spoke distinctly.

"I praise the Lord this afternoon for what He means to me," he said, "If I've ever stood in the way of any of you here, please forgive me."

A man near the rostrum turned toward the rear, paused and spoke slowly: "Most of you have heard of the prodigal son. I've been down in the hog pen eating with the hogs. Now I'm up at the table."

One revivalist injected a touch of humor in his testimony: "I ought to send the Devil a get-well card, since he's probably sick today! The Devil has given me a hard time and I'm glad to be giving him one now."

A girl seated near the front, stood and said, "I was a cheerleader in high school and now I'm rooting for the most wonderful team in the world."

Six women students entered the auditorium and seated themselves near the back; Dr. Kenyon pointed them out and said: "We'll start taking your testimony right down the line." All six testified. (Incidently, they had prayed in their rooms that if the Lord wanted them to witness for Him, they would if given a chance. Their chance was given as soon as they entered the building and were seated.)

Another six young women walked to the stage and sang their testimonies as a sextet, their voices blending in these words:

"Nobody compares with Jesus. No one so near; no one so dear as He. Jesus alone can take my sadness and give me a wonderful peace."

Some women participants broke into tears at the end of their declarations, but all were firm in their recited convictions.

These testimonies were taken from the Asbury Collegian (Revival Edition), published on March 4, 1950:

Betty Wheatley, Freshman: I definitely believe the revival started because of the prayers of the many groups and the petitions of many students in their devotions. The one special thing God did for me was to cause me to trust Him more and to wait on Him. He also caused me to feel more deeply the need of prayer.

Ron Carter, Freshman: Ten months ago the Lord lifted me out of a world of sin. I was a rather wild fellow and did a lot of things I should not have done, but He gave me real peace in my heart. I felt that I was growing in grace but never realized before this revival just how far I was going in grace. I never thought I would shout, but I have done quite a bit of that during this revival. I feel a call to the ministry, and the Lord has foretold to me two things during this revival, and they both happened.

Judy Kuhn, Junior: Like everyone else I think the revival definitely came from prayer and was sent of God. Although I haven't had any overwhelming feeling, I have learned to trust the

Lord far more than I ever realized was possible. I know now what living by faith means. "He knoweth the way that I take and when He hath tried me I shall come forth as gold." - Job 23: 10.

Bob Barefoot, Senior: Since I have been in Asbury College, the Devil has tried to tell me many times, "Give up, Bob. There's no use to keep on praying. There is no use to keep on believing holiness." In the first place I had a hard time getting into Asbury; sickness, discouragement from home, and everything else tried to get me to give up; but I held on in prayer and leaned on the everlasting arms of Jesus. Since this revival, I have found out that it pays to serve Jesus and keep true to Him, for He is in the prayer answering business and He will never fail. I praise Him for about forty-five answers to prayer. I believe this revival came because a group of us got together and prayed it down.

On August 23, 1956, Bob Barefoot was taken home to heaven as a result of an auto-truck collision near Marshall, North Carolina, where he was on his way home from attending a meeting nearby.

The night before the calamity, Bob sang two special numbers, the first entitled, "The Name of Jesus," before which he said, "This is my testimony," and the second was, "Face to Face with Christ My Saviour." Miss Dorothy Raub, the evangelist, then preached on the subject of death, stressing its certainly, impartiality, and nearness. The next day the tragedy occurred.

Following the accident, Bob regained consciousness sufficiently at the hospital to recognize his district superintendent, Dr. J. W. Fitzgerald, and to quote one Psalm after another, particularly Psalms 23 and 121. Just before he passed away, Bob spelled out the word "heaven" and said, "It is beautiful! I wish Louise was here." She joined him in the Church Triumphant the following day.

Rose Whitehead, Freshman: Truly I think the revival started by prayer. I have never been so blessed in my life as I have during this revival. Some people have made decisions now which will affect their whole lives and the world too. I thank the Lord that I am privileged to be at Asbury during this revival and feel that I have grown closer to Him.

Roberto Lenz, (Cuba), Sophomore: I think that by the power of God, prayers of students and of professors of this institution this revival started. This has been a time of great spiritual refreshing for me. It is beyond me to express how I feel deeply in my heart. I praise the Lord every day for having led me to Asbury, for I have received such a blessing, not only because of the good education but also because of the good spiritual atmosphere. I love the Lord with all my heart, and my goal in life is to serve Him in my own country. Praise to His name for the revival.

Marilyn Loy, Sophomore: I praise the Lord for reclaiming me a week ago last Thursday and for the opportunity of going home last weekend and testifying to my family and church. I am glad that we can have victory in Jesus. It is real and will never lose its power. "Thou hast made known to me the ways of life: Thou shalt make me full of joy with Thy countenance." Acts 2:28.

Jean Spahr, Junior: Praise the Lord for sanctifying a dyed-in-the-wool Calvinist. I was determined to stay a good Calvinist but my life was in need of a greater power -- the power of the Holy Spirit. I wrote to my family back home and to my pastor, who is a Presbyterian, and pray that the Lord will use my letters to show them this wonderful way of holiness.

Eldon Raymond, Freshman: I think definitely this revival was of God. My name for it is "spontaneous combustion." God worked everything up to a head and let it blow. I think it was definitely because of prayer. God has been wanting to give it to us for a long time. My prayer is that it will continue until every person on Asbury's campus will know Christ in His saving and sanctifying power. I believe this revival and the publicity it was given by the papers and over the television has been God's own way of reaching souls that might never have been reached otherwise. I thank God that He has shown me more the need of prayer and also thank Him for being able to preach a gospel that can be lived.

Bob Havens, Senior: I went through Asbury four years and had no idea what a religious experience was. I started coming to chapel to see what it was all about until I became miserable. One night I didn't go to sleep all night because I was afraid the Lord would come. Although I was reared in a preacher's family I became hardened, and would not accept the Lord because I was afraid He would make me give up my roller skates and I wanted to be a professional skater. Saturday night I was saved -- not because of all the people's talking, but I respected Dr. Corbitt, who showed me that everyone had ambitions. When I went to the altar I had so many confessions to make they burdened me down. Thank God I have Him in my heart now, and I don't think this revival will ever end when we can have the Lord.

Henry C. James, resident of Wilmore: On Saturday night, February 25, I made my way to Hughes Auditorium curious to know what was taking place there. After reading the papers and hearing about what was going on, I had to see it to believe it.

Previous to this, I rarely darkened a church door. However, as I entered the building and reached the top of the balcony stairs, I had the most unusual feeling as I sensed a drawing power that swept over me in such a way it is hard to explain. This was the most positive witness to me that this revival was not of human origin.

A short time later I reluctantly went down to the altar. It was there I had the struggle of my life. I prayed for some three hours. I was literally exhausted when I finally broke through the barrier that separated me from the Saviour. It seems that I could not muster enough faith to believe the Lord could save a sinner like me.

After the midnight hour the Lord met my need. I shall ever praise Him for His matchless love and mercy in that He gave His Son to redeem an unworthy sinner.

Then followed another soul struggle about the call to preach. This was the last thing that I desired to do. However, two days later I gave myself for Him to use my life as He pleased.

Satan had stained my soul with sin, but Jesus washed it "white as snow." The devil had long enslaved my soul and darkness blinded my life, but Christ set me free and gave me the light of full salvation.

As I live this life I want it to be the shout of my soul from now throughout all eternity, "If the Son, therefore, shall make you free, ye shall be free indeed." - John 8:36.

Peace and joy have taken the place of turmoil and strife. Satan is ever seeking to regain my soul: but when he comes to tempt me, the Saviour is ever present to vindicate the precious promises to me in His Holy Word.

Unfortunately since the meeting there have been some who witnessed the power of God but have been deceived by Satan and have fallen away. However, even these cannot deny that the presence of God was in the meetings and that God dealt with their hearts. Nevertheless, the fact that some have fallen does not in the least reflect on the dealings of the Holy Spirit.

The Asbury Collegian (Revival Edition), of March 4, carried this statement:

And still the revival continues! That it is a direct answer to prayer no one can deny. The need was immense, spiritual life on the campus was at a low ebb. Then God's Spirit fell searching, convicting, converting, purifying, reviving. Some were saved, others received calls into missionary or other full-time Christian service. Whether with tears or happy shouts or merely a radiant smile, young and old arose from the altar with the witness within that all was right with their souls. To all walking in obedience with the will of God came a new vision, a greater determination to proclaim Christ, and a clearer conception of the Christian's power in prayer!

ONE YEAR LATER

George Reynolds, staff writer for the Lexington Herald, visited the campus one year later and had this to say:

Students and faculty members of Asbury College today had happy but solemn memories of the great spontaneous revival which started on their campus a year ago and continued for five days and nights.

Everyone was aware of the anniversary today, but there was no movement to rekindle the dramatic demonstrations of religious zeal which last year gained nation-wide interest and brought hundreds of people here to testify of their renewed faith in God.

The sunshine-brightened campus was quiet today, with students slowly walking to and from classes and several small boys playing ball on the front lawn. Two students strolled from a building with their parents, showing them the sights. Occasional laughter burst from open windows of classrooms.

At Hughes Memorial Auditorium, where a student arose during chapel exercises last February 23 and asked to testify, launching the greatest revival in the school's history, two caretakers cleaned and adjusted seats in preparation for tonight's showing of a junior class play.

The junior class play also had been scheduled that night a year ago, but devout students filled the auditorium to capacity, many remaining there all night to pray, to sing and to testify.

Dean Jay B. Kenyon today smiled as he recalled that proceeds from last year's play were to have been used for remodeling work on the school's original building, which was being converted into a museum. When the play was postponed, he said he decided to "pass the hat" among the revivalists so that the class fund-raising work would not be in vain.

When the offering was tabulated, it was found that contributions exceeded even the fondest hopes of the play's sponsors.

Dean Kenyon emphasized today that nobody

expected a renewal of the revival on its anniversary, because it was not an organized service, and participants had no intention of creating an annual observance.

The now-famous revival rapidly grew in intensity and size after it began at Thursday-morning chapel services. By Saturday, it had become nation-wide in interest, and reporters, photographers and radio-television personnel flocked to the auditorium to describe the activities.

Throughout its course, worshippers displayed genuine solemnity. While some testified, others sat in quiet meditation.

Dean Kenyon, left in charge of the college while President Z. T. Johnson conducted a revival in Florida, was bombarded with telephone calls and wires from all over the country.

Later, letters from Asbury Alumni all over the world told of reading reports of the revival. Newspapers as far away as England carried stories about it.

People from all parts of Kentucky and surrounding states came here to participate.

Many reporters, unaccustomed to describing such a service, found it difficult to find adequate words to express the deep impression it made on them.

Each night there were indications that the revival might end. But small groups of students, townspeople and outsiders remained, usually in silent prayer. While some rested, others carried on. President Johnson wired from Florida, asking that the revival continue until he could return.

Finally, on Sunday, Dean Kenyon ordered college classes to resume on Tuesday morning, and at 7:00 a. m. Tuesday, the last three worshippers left the auditorium. (There were services which continued in the evenings for guidance.)

Students were reminded of the revival's anniversary at chapel exercises yesterday, but all of them seemed to realize that such a movement could not recur on schedule, Dean Kenyon said.

Betty Brown, a student from Nashville, Tennessee, best explained their attitude.

"We could try again and again," she said, "but it would never be the same."

The extent of the influence of the revival will never be known until the revelation of God. One thing we can be sure of is that the results were positive and a large percentage of those who dedicated themselves will remain vital Christian workers. This movement was deeply felt by all in attendance at the services. The testimonies were heart-centered and clear-cut.

Dean Kenyon asked the students if they would remain in Christian service.

When he asked those with affirmative intentions to stand, 600 rose in unison.

Christian service would mean the ministry, missionaries or service in hospitals or similar work.

SEVEN YEARS LATER

Almost seven years have passed since the Asbury revival began. Dr. T. M. Anderson gives a summary of his evangelistic efforts since the meeting. These experiences are no doubt the result of the power of God and the leadership of the Holy Spirit as was the college revival.

The great revival broke out spontaneously at Asbury College in 1950, on the morning of February 23. What little preaching was done during that great visitation from God was my responsibility, but it was not much more than to give an exhortation, for the Spirit of God moved in great power upon the student body and upon the visitors, many of whom came from hundreds of miles. I want, as part of the record, to include what I saw that followed that gracious visitation of God.

I preached my last message of the revival on Friday night and on Saturday, with a group of students, went to Jackson, Mississippi, where an urgent call had been made because the revival had broken out there through the testimony of Rev. Marvin Osbourne and his wife, who were students at Asbury College but lived in Jackson, Mississippi. We went to the Wells Memorial Methodist Church, where I spoke for the first time on the Sabbath. I do not think I shall ever forget the crowd of people who came, although there was very little advertising regarding the meeting. They filled the sanctuary, the vestibules, all the standing room, and some young people even climbed into the windows in the basement in order to get into the service. The police had to direct traffic, for the cars were parked on many of the streets almost as far as one could see. The meeting ran with such force and momentum that we did not close on Sunday night as had been expected, but continued over the next week. I was released from my classes and continued there in the ministry of the word. Then the revival broke out from there in Hattiesburg, Mississippi, where some of the boys did part of the preaching. I preached there two nights and the rest of the time at the Wells Memorial Methodist Church.

We went out one day to a Negro school called Piney Woods, and I spoke about twenty minutes in the morning chapel service. The Spirit of God fell on the colored people, ranging in age from sixteen to nineteen. There must have been 250 or 300 of them that crowded around the front. I never heard such weeping, praying, and seeking God; seldom have I witnessed anything like this visitation of God that came upon them.

Then I returned to the college and asked Dr. Johnson whether he would kindly release me for the three months of the spring quarter so that I could carry that message with which my soul was burning and give it in as many places as God would open for me. This permission he readily granted, but he asked me whether I had any calls at that time. I told him that I did not have any then, but that I was to go for two days to a preachers' meeting in Cincinnati, Ohio. This was between quarters and these were the only calls I had at present. He then said, "We will release you, but unless you have some income from your work, we will pay your salary while you go and testify. You can take up any freewill offerings and repay the college." That was on a Monday or Tuesday morning. When I returned home after my visit to his office, my phone began to ring, and within a few hours I had enough calls from churches in many states to run until summer. God suddenly opened the doors to go to churches from California to the Pacific Northwest for one day, two days, or any time I could give them.

I went to the two days preachers' meeting in Shreveport, Louisiana, in the First Nazarene Church. The people came in such crowds that it was almost impossible to get through into the church. They sought God by the hundreds. From there revivals broke out in many of the other churches.

The same thing was true when I went to the preachers' meeting in Cincinnati, Ohio. There was one night the church was so crowded that strong men had to make a way through the crowd to get me to the pulpit to preach. Many people sought God here. From there I went for three days to a very gracious visitation of God in the Nazarene school in Bethany, Oklahoma. Then I traveled through Oklahoma, Texas, Arkansas, Tennessee, Kentucky, Virginia, and West Virginia.

One thing of interest to me was that when I would travel by plane and would speak with passengers or to the stewardesses, I noticed that if I asked, "Have you heard of the great revival at Asbury College?" and if the person said, "Yes, tell me about it," almost without exception, I could get that one to Christ.

My first campmeeting following these week end meetings was held during the latter part of June and the first part of July, 1950, in Alexandria, Louisiana. I had the responsibility of doing most of the preaching. I recall that at the first Sunday evening service I was to preach, and I had read the text in Hebrews 2:1 - "We ought to give the more earnest heed to the things which we have heard, lest at any time we should let them slip." I suppose I had been preaching for about ten minutes, when the Holy Ghost fell on that audience of perhaps a thousand or more people and swept over them like wind that sweeps over a field of ripened grain. They began to come to the altar and some prayed all night.

Then on Tuesday in the evening service while I was praying, the Holy Ghost came on the audience again and they made their way to the altar in great numbers to seek God. I saw strong young men just dive at the altar. It is estimated that during the ten days of that camp more than a thousand people sought God.

I then went to the great campmeeting at Indian Springs, Georgia. I was associated with Dr. McPheeters and with Dr. Sprague, a pastor from Evansville, Indiana. On the first Saturday night I was to preach and I had the people stand while I prayed before the sermon. Once again, I saw a manifestation of the Spirit of God, that fell upon that vast audience in great power. Someone estimated that there were between seventy-five and one hundred people who came immediately to the altar without any invitation seeking God.

Then in August I went to a district campmeeting of the Nazarene Church. The same gracious manifestation of God accompanied that meeting as people sought God. The Spirit of God would fall upon them in mighty power, sweep them to the altar, and cause some to pray all night.

I saw the work of the Master in many very remarkable instances throughout the year that followed the gracious revival at Asbury College. I kept some account of those meetings, and it is my estimate that there were somewhere between fourteen and sixteen thousand people.

I noticed that three things aided in bringing a mighty visitation of God: that people find a place to pray in the early morning, that those knowing there was more for them in the grace of God respond promptly to the Spirit, and that churches desist from too many programs and too much ritual and give God a chance to use earnest prayer and simple messages to manifest His power. One instance that illustrates the importance of these points occurred while I was in that very gracious meeting at Wells Memorial Methodist Church in Jackson, Mississippi. On Sunday morning when I had preached on entire sanctification and had made the altar call, which was simply an appeal to any that wanted the blessing of holiness to step out on their own volition and seek the Lord, the altar soon filled. A pastor that I knew quite well and who had come three hundred miles to be in the services asked me, "What can I do in my church to see such a visitation of God?"

I replied, "Go home and tell the church people that you will have service tomorrow night. Don't announce any preaching. Then each night have no program; follow the leadings of the Spirit; sing, pray, testify; but be perfectly free, and merely let the Spirit of God have a chance." I said this to him because many times we've had so much program we've prevented God from really working the way He desires.

That pastor went home and did as I told him. His meeting broke out and ran for three weeks with hundreds of people seeking God. People would leave their homes at two o'clock in the morning to come to the church, where there was a praying group of people, and there seek the Lord.

Thus, I have found what apparently, is the secret of hearing from God. We have too much program and too little place for God. We should meet in simple faith, sing the old hymns, get people into the attitude of worship, and have them pray in the early hours while their minds are fresh and clear. If they will do that, they will see marvelous manifestations of God. Furthermore, I noticed what I thought to be some accompaniments of these revivals; frequently people would be suddenly healed of some serious disease. The healing did not seem to be an answer to prayer, for it did not seem that we were especially thinking of people being healed. They were just healed because of their faith as persons were in Bible times.

These are a few of the incidents which proved that if there is faith to believe we can have in this day marvelous visitations of God. Now almost seven years have passed since the Asbury revival; during these years I have ministered in conventions, in holiness campmeetings, in assemblies, and in preachers' meetings, and I have seen twenty-five or thirty thousand people seek God. Everywhere that I have preached I have urged the necessity of simple faith, devout prayers.

With these conditions met, we can have a visitation of God. My heart is set against a kind of a professional ministry that has just so many sermons to preach and so many songs to sing and a certain program to be rigidly followed. We don't mean to shove the Holy Spirit away, we don't mean to crowd Him out; but we do it nevertheless with a great many of these programs and human plans. We overlook the necessity of absolute and complete dependence on the Holy Ghost.

Thus, we have seen, at least in part, just what can happen even today when the Spirit of God is honored and given His rightful place in the lives of Christian people. May the power of that mighty movement of God which began on the campus of Asbury College and spread rapidly, never die. May these fires burn brightly and kindle more fires. May we give our first allegiance to Christ and to the advancement of His kingdom on earth. We would share with all the world the glorious revelation of Divine power manifest to God's people.

SOURCES

Blakely, Mary Lee, (Courier-Journal Staff Writer), "The Revival at Asbury Follows An Old Pattern, The Courier-Journal, Section 1, Louisville, Kentucky.

Gibson, John, (Associated Press Staff Writer), "Townspeople and Teachers Join in as Asbury College Revival Continues, IX, No. 56, The Courier-Journal, February 24, 1950, Louisville, Kentucky

Holland, William W., "The Asbury College Revival," The Pentecostal Herald, March 15, 1950, I, No. 44, Louisville, Kentucky.

Leavens, Edwin T., (Editor), "Impressions of Asbury Revival as Witnessed by Editor," The Community News - Lexington's Weekly Newspaper, Friday, March 3, 1950, I, No. 44, Lexington, Kentucky.

Lewyn, Jack, (reporter), "Asbury Student Revival Fervor Continues Strong," The Herald-Leader, February 25, 1950, Lexington, Kentucky.

Lewyn, Jack, (reporter), "Revival at Asbury Continues Into Fifth Day," The Lexington Herald, February 27, 1950, Lexington, Kentucky.

Looney, Ralph, "Prayers and Testimonials Continue as Spiritual Revival Sways Students," The Lexington Leader, February 25, 1950, LXII, No. 48, Lexington, Kentucky.

McPheeters, Julian C., "The Asbury Revival Abides," The Pentecostal Herald, December 6, 1950, II, No. 1.

Mavis, W. Curry, (editor), "Revival Tides Are Rising," The Christian Minister, April, 1950, II, No. 1.

Monson, W. D., "Asbury Students Carry on Revival Past 100th Hour," The Lexington Leader, (UP), February 28, 1950, Lexington, Kentucky.

Reister, Joe, (Staff Correspondent), "Asbury Revival Likely to go Several Days," The Courier-Journal, February 25, 1950, Louisville, Kentucky.

Reynolds, George, (Herald Staff Writer), "Anniversary of Spontaneous Asbury Revival Noted Quietly by College Student Body," The Lexington Herald, February 24, 1951, Lexington, Kentucky

Shirer, Robert, (editor), The Asbury Collegian, (Revival Edition), XXXIII, No. 18, Wilmore, Kentucky.

MISCELLANEOUS ARTICLES

Anonymous, "Weary Students Continue 78-Hour Revival," February 26, 1950.

Anonymous, "Asbury Revival Shows No Indication of Ending." Associated Press, February 26, 1950.

Asbury Alumnus and Asbury College Bulletin, "The Asbury Revival," January 1950 - June 1955, February 1950. Wilmore, Kentucky.

Christian Advocate, "Evangelism: Revival for 114 Hours," March 16, 1950, Chicago, Illinois.

Courier-Journal, (Associated Press), "Students Renew Revival After Hour's Suspension," February 26, (Vol. 191), No. 57, Louisville, Kentucky.

Dallas Morning News, (Associated Press), "College Revival Turns Marathon," February 25, 1950.

The Lexington Leader, "Three Asbury Students to Hold
  Revival in Mississippi," March 1, 1950.

For remarks and additional copies
write: Asbury Seminary Bookstore
Wilmore, Kentucky

www.ingramcontent.com/pod-product-compliance
Lightning Source LLC
Chambersburg PA
CBHW020515030426
42337CB00011B/407